A PORTFOLIO OF

DECK
IDEAS

CREATIVE
PUBLISHING
international

MINNETONKA, MINNESOTA

CONTENTS

Copyright © 1993
Creative Publishing international
5900 Green Oak Drive
Minnetonka, Minnesota 55343
1-800-328-3895

CREATIVE PUBLISHING international

President/CEO: David D. Murphy
Vice President/Editor-in-Chief: Patricia K. Jacobsen
Vice President/Retail Sales & Marketing: Richard M. Miller

Library of Congress
Cataloging-in-Publication Data
A Portfolio of Deck Ideas

        p. cm
    ISBN 0-86573-922-6 (softcover)
    1. Decks (Architecture, Domestic) — Design and construction.
    I. Creative Publishing international, Inc. II. Title: Deck ideas.
TH4970.P68 1993
721'.84—dc20   93-8175

Author: Home How-To Institute™
Creative Director: William B. Jones
Editorial Director: Bryan Trandem
Project Director: Paul Currie
Art Director: Catherine Achhamer
Project Manager: Carol Harvatin
Writer: Carol Harvatin
Editor: Bryan Trandem

Copy Editor: Janice Cauley
Production Staff: Catherine Achhamer,
    Julie Sutphen
Vice President of Development
    Planning & Production: Jim Bindas
Production Manager: Amelia Merz

Printed on American paper by :
R.R. Donnelley & Sons Co.

10 9 8 7 6 5 4

Other Porftolio of Ideas books include:

A Portfolio of Kitchen Ideas
A Portfolio of Deck Ideas
A Portfolio of Landscape Ideas
A Portfolio of Bathroom Ideas
A Portfolio of Window & Window Treatment Ideas
A Portfolio of Flooring Ideas
A Portfolio of Bedroom Ideas
A Portfolio of Unique Deck Ideas
A Portfolio of Lighting Ideas
A Portfolio of Water Garden & Specialty Landscape Ideas
A Portfolio of Porch & Patio Ideas
A Portfolio of Storage Ideas
A Portfolio of Fireplace Ideas
A Portfolio of Ceramic & Natural Tile Ideas
A Portfolio of Fence & Gate Ideas
A Portfolio of Outdoor Furnishing Ideas
A Portfolio of Home Spa Ideas
A Portfolio of Home Office Ideas
A Portfolio of Home Entertainment Ideas

Photos on cover courtesy of California Redwood Association (Left); Milt Charno and Associates (Top right)

Photo courtesy of Milt Charno & Associates

▲ **This multilevel deck** *turns a steep, rocky, unusable hillside into an attractive and very usable outdoor living area. The top level can be used for lounging and sunbathing, the middle for dining and socializing, and the lower level doubles as a step leading to the yard.*

What makes a great deck?

A great deck is an outdoor living area that functions as an extension of your home. It accommodates your family's life-style with flexibility for socializing, recreation or relaxation. A great deck turns an ordinary yard into a beautiful showplace.

To inspire you with ideas for creating your perfect deck, we have gathered over 150 stunning color photographs of spectacular deck designs and features and compiled them in *A Portfolio of Deck Ideas.*

In the first section you will discover how to make the most effective use of your existing space. Many elements included in outdoor living areas are multifunctional. Fences, arbors and trellises add visual interest and help to manage sun, wind and rain. Built-in benches can be used as storage bins, and flower boxes with wide edges double as seating. Style and design ideas for gazebos, benches, steps, railings and flower boxes are shown throughout.

The second part of the book is a portfolio of more than 50 color photographs of fabulous showcase decks. Gorgeous single-level and multilevel designs offer ideas to help you design a deck that suits your family's specific needs.

Whether you are adding a simple platform outside your back door or designing a multilevel masterpiece, this book is full of creative and practical ideas to help you design a great deck.

Photo courtesy of P & M Cedar Products, Inc.

▲ **This large, contemporary deck** *has three distinct activity areas: an open, spacious social center, a separate dining area, and space for an elevated hot tub. A low bench defines the angles of the deck and leads the eye to the raised area around the hot tub.*

▲ **Small but elaborate**, this redwood deck makes efficient use of space by building around an existing tree that provides shade and adds an interesting focal point. An overhead arbor also shelters users from the sun and creates a link between deck and house. Simple wooden benches provide seating and create a boundary for the deck.

◄ **A simple line** with an elegant design style is consistent throughout this multilevel redwood deck. Seen in the open railings and flower boxes, these elements help emphasize the various levels that divide the areas of this deck.

▲ **The basic lines** and shapes in this deck add visual interest and guide the eye. Contrasting decking patterns emphasize the change in levels between two deck areas.

PLANNING
Flexibility for many functions

When designing your deck, plan so that "form follows function." First determine what you want to use your deck for, then plan a deck to meet all your family's needs in one attractive form.

Be sure your deck will accommodate a variety of activities including cooking and dining, sunbathing, playing games and entertaining. Also include areas for shade, relaxation and privacy.

Be generous with space and plan your activity areas so that one doesn't interfere with another. Traffic patterns can be controlled by using features like steps, railings and planter boxes to create walkways.

▲ **This deck/walkway** controls the flow of traffic and provides areas for comfortable relaxation. The angled benches with attached planter boxes also create attractive, visual lines.

▼ **The activity alcove** created by combining a raised platform with an overhead arbor provides a shady play area or a quiet, out-of-the-way retreat.

▲ **A built-in bench** saves space and supplies seating. The decorative, open-weave pattern of the railings encloses the space but doesn't confine the user.

▲ *The angles and shape* of the upper level on this deck are repeated in the contour of the bench on the lower level. *The different levels function as distinct activity areas separated by railings, steps and benches.*

▲ *A terraced deck* allows users to enjoy the outdoors with an unrestricted view. The dining area is bordered on three sides by a raised level that leads into the house.

Sets of stairs can be sculptural links between levels and activity areas. This wide, open stairway guides traffic from an upper-level dining area to a larger entertaining area on a lower level. The vertical balusters of the railings give the deck a formal look and design continuity throughout. ▶

▲ **This deck wraps around** the house for easy access from anywhere inside. The shape of the deck, with its curved corners and smooth, continuous line of low benches and flower boxes, complements the shape of the house. A set of wide steps leads from the deck to a ground-level patio.

PLANNING

A smooth transition from indoors to outdoors

A social gathering moves easily from indoors to outdoors when a comfortable deck welcomes you into a lush, open-air living space. To get maximum enjoyment from this natural extension of indoor space, you must consider all elements of your yard, as well as your personal likes and dislikes.

Outdoor rooms are more comfortable when they are divided into several smaller areas. The deck ideas in this book are excellent examples of how to create comfortable, usable living space in almost any outdoor environment.

Both architecturally and aesthetically, the materials, colors and textures used for your deck should complement and harmonize with those in your house and landscape.

An open platform deck snugs up to this house and helps soften the stark transition from the predominantly vertical, angular slope of the house to the horizontal flatness of the yard. The simple design of this platform deck complements the contemporary style of the house. ▶

Photo courtesy of Western Wood Products

▲ **Angled benches** *follow the contours of this single-level deck, creating efficient living space from a shallow lawn surrounded by thick trees. The wide bench style provides a visual break between the ground-level deck and the dense foliage.*

▼ *A colorful flower garden frames this simple, two-level platform deck. An L-shaped bench on the outside edge of the top level encloses the area and defines the boundaries of this charming outdoor setting.*

Photo courtesy of Georgia-Pacific Corporation

Photo courtesy of Southern Pine Marketing Council

▲ **An open, airy platform deck** *with tiered stairs rises gradually to the door level. It provides a wide, unobstructed surface with plenty of seating on the wide steps.*

9

▲ **An elegant gazebo** *adds a charming, shady sanctuary to an outdoor entertainment area. Built-in benches and flower boxes form an inviting path, leading to the steps of the gazebo.*

▲ **This custom design** *features a sunken garden as the focal point. A terraced deck/walkway surrounding three sides is combined with a low bench built around the ground level to create a frame for the garden.*

▲ **Careful attention to design elements,** *like the details in the railings, adds charm to this multilevel, multifunctional deck.*

PLANNING

Focus on special features

Gazebos, overhead arbors, vertical trellises, flower boxes, hot tubs and fences are special features that add visual appeal and value to your outdoor living space. Even common deck elements, like steps, benches, and railings can be special features if they feature an unusual design.

Photo courtesy of Georgia-Pacific Corporation

▲ *A **built-in bench** provides plenty of seating without using much space. An attached railing adds a comfortable back for the bench.*

Photo courtesy of Archadeck

▲ *The **hot tub** on this deck is surrounded by a raised deck, for seating or sunbathing. A planter box built around an existing tree also provides a shady place to sit.*

DESIGN

Simply stated or dramatically detailed

Subtle touches can make the difference in the finished look of a deck. The shape of the deck itself, the decking patterns, and the styling of rails, stairs and other design attributes play a big part in the finished look of your deck and help unite it with your home.

The size of a deck and its surroundings will determine what kinds of design features to include. Small decks in limited spaces should include a limited number of multifunctional elements, like built-in benches that can also be used for storage, or planter boxes and steps that add seating. Large decks should use structural elements like railings, arbors and trellises to break up the space and make it more visually appealing.

Photo courtesy of Weyerhaeuser

▲ *The herringbone pattern* used in an overhead arbor helps diffuse sunlight and casts a textured shadow pattern on the deck below.

Photo courtesy of Archadeck

▲ *The contemporary design,* featuring crisp, white vertical railings, gives this deck a fresh, clean look.

▲ **The elegance** of this stately home is complemented by the stylish deck design. The simple lines and sleek styles seen in the benches and steps work beautifully to unify the deck, pool and house.

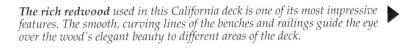

▲ **Open-weave construction** of the overhead arbor adds interesting shadow patterns and reduces the effects of the sun's rays on the deck below. Lattice is also used as an attractive screen to hide an unsightly area underneath the deck.

The rich redwood used in this California deck is one of its most impressive features. The smooth, curving lines of the benches and railings guide the eye over the wood's elegant beauty to different areas of the deck. ▶

DESIGN

Bring a new dimension to your domain

▲ **The natural elements** *surrounding this redwood deck help dictate the unique shape of the ground-level platform. The weblike pattern used in the decking and the angles of the railings visually extend the deck between the trees.*

▶ **The asymmetrical angles** of the railing are repeated in the built-in bench to give a continuous line that defines the edge of this deck. The wide, low bench also serves as a railing that doesn't obstruct the view.

◀ **A specific theme** can be created by using elements that have a distinct design style. The pagoda design used in these matching arbors gives an oriental flavor to this outdoor space.

▲ **Large three-tiered deck** *creates a comfortable social gathering area on the edge of a sprawling lawn. An open platform style makes it easily accessible. This deck helps to divide this large, grassy space into smaller, more useable areas.*

▼ **An elaborate overhead** *arbor with a lowered ceiling creates an intimate alcove within the larger deck setting. Steps leading into a sunken area are also used as seating.*

Design

A well-designed deck uses its environment to create beautiful settings and valuable living space from previously unused land.

Large spaces are divided into smaller areas that are more comfortable and versatile, either by separating deck areas with design elements, or with multiple levels. Steep slopes and otherwise rough terrain can be transformed into functional living areas by using creative deck designs.

Photo courtesy of Milt Charno & Associates

▲ **The underside** of this cantilevered deck is paneled for a rich, finished appearance. The same finished style is carried throughout the entire deck. Contrasting stains are used as a design element.

▲ **Two existing trees** are incorporated into this unique deck. A striking starburst decking pattern is featured in a raised platform area.

Photo courtesy of Caddcon Inc.

▼ **This outdoor area** is divided by the distinct angles of the vertical railing. The attractive railing encompasses a dining and entertainment area, then continues around the hot tub setting. A raised platform and overhead arbor provide privacy for hot tub users.

Photo courtesy of Southern Pine Marketing Council

▲ **The layered design** of the railing, and the flared shape of the steps as they wrap around the hot tub, add visual interest and complement the wood lap siding of the house.

▲ **The staircase** includes a large landing that divides the staircase into balanced areas. The middle landing allows the stairway to follow the contours of the slope.

▶ **The size** of the lower-level platform of this deck is proportional to the larger second level. The shape and angles of the lower-level bench reflect the same shapes and angles seen in the steps and railings around the upper level.

DESIGN
Balance and Proportion

To achieve balance within a deck environment, integrate design elements for a clear, consistent look throughout the deck. When designing an outdoor living area, it is important to create a comfortable relationship between the planes of the intended floor and walls in the open space. The deck area should feel enclosed but not confining. Complete the feeling of balance by keeping all elements in proportion to your house and the other structures in your yard.

▲ **The raised deck** that extends from the back was built large enough to balance the expansive size of this house. The rustic design of the house is complemented by the rough, sturdy deck.

Wide, low steps keep an open feel to this deck even though walls of the house surround it on three sides. The design of the decking, and the shape and size of the deck itself, work to visually hold back the imposing walls and establish a comfortable, open-air room. ▶

Photo courtesy of California Redwood Association

Sun/Shade

Natural climate control for your deck

▲ *Natural shade trees* are used on this poolside deck to create a cool retreat from the heat of the sun. A flat, open platform located away from the dining area is a perfect place for sunbathing.

Whether you're a sun worshipper or a shade dweller, a versatile deck offers something for everyone. Overhead arbors are a simple, elegant way to cool off a sunny area on your deck. Vertical trellises and screens also have a charming appeal. Open-weave style arbors and trellises provide shade and allow air circulation through the lattice. To determine placement of these structures, observe the migration of the sun across your deck and note its location at peak-use periods of the day. Take advantage of natural shade givers, such as trees and large bushes. These natural elements can be incorporated as part of your deck design to help control comfort in your outdoor living area.

▶ *A retreat unto itself,* this raised deck area has a sunny area for hot tub users and a shady dining area sheltered by a large arbor overhead.

Photo courtesy of California Redwood Association

▲ **Another way** to filter out the sun's rays is to use a screen as part of your vertical or overhead structure. A thin, light screen attached to the arbor or trellis lets in plenty of light but keeps the area cool.

◀ **The design** of the arbor above creates a nice shadow pattern on the floor of this delightful deck. The multilevels provide areas for food preparation, intimate gatherings and sunning.

◀◀ **An overhead arbor** links the existing trees with the deck and the house and creates a sheltered dining area. The large tree in the center creates shady spots in other areas of the deck.

SUN/SHADE

There are many attractive and effective options for controlling sun and shade. Trellises, arbors and gazebos offer maximum impact in a minimum amount of space. The charm of an overhead arbor is enhanced by the fascinating shadows cast by the unique shapes and patterns. The perfect spot for relaxation, a graceful gazebo is an interesting focal point for any deck.

▲ *The unique design* of this overhead structure creates a comfortable retreat from the heat. It uses widely spaced wooden strips for the roof construction, which allows cooling breezes to circulate through the structure.

▲ *A large, open arbor* provides scattered shade patterns that diffuse the brightness of the sun's light around this poolside deck area.

Photo courtesy of P & M Cedar Products, Inc.

Photo courtesy of Weyerhaeuser

▲ *The importance of paying attention* to *design details is evident in the beautiful silhouette of this deck at sunset.*

▲ *Enjoy the outdoors*, *no matter what the weather. From inside the shelter of a screened porch, you can walk out to either a shady corner of the deck, or an open, sunny area.*

▼ *A sunny poolside area* is *surrounded by an elevated observation deck. The shady area under the deck can be used as a comfortable spot to cool off. The upper deck also blocks the heat from the downstairs area inside the house and keeps it cool.*

Photo courtesy of P & M Cedar Products, Inc.

▲ *A charming waterside gazebo extends an invitation for intimate dining. This freestanding structure serves as a place to enjoy a warm sunset after supper or as a sheltered retreat from rain and sun.*

GAZEBOS

From Simple to Sophisticated

Gazebos are a great way to add dimension and give an elegant touch to your outdoor living area. In addition to their graceful appearance, multifunctional gazebos increase the versatility of your deck. A gazebo can act as an outdoor den, an alfresco dining area or a private, romantic hot tub setting.

Photo courtesy of Milt Charno & Associates

▶ **This gazebo** *has a solid roof and completely screened walls to shelter users from sun, rain and insects.*

Photo opposite page courtesy of Caddcon Designs ▲

Photo courtesy of Milt Charno & Associates

▲ *A **lattice gazebo roof** casts interesting shadow patterns. The open-weave design allows a breeze to circulate and the open walls are consistent with the airy look of the roof.*

Photo courtesy of Archadeck

Photo courtesy of Southern Pine Marketing Council

▲ **This unusual gazebo design** has the feel of a primitive hut. A connected deckway leads to the detached area of the ground-level deck to create a quiet resting area.

◄ **This semi-enclosed, freestanding gazebo** creates a cool, secluded retreat in a shady, wooded area.

Photo courtesy of Milt Charno & Associates

▲ **The design detail** of this gazebo gives a formal look to this deck setting. The vertical boards used in the gazebo design create a visual style compatible with the design of the railings.

Photo courtesy of Western Wood Products

Photo courtesy of Archadeck

▲ *A gazebo built over* an extended area of the deck has a solid roof that shelters a hot tub. This roof provides partial seclusion and shelters users from the elements.

◀ *Cedar shingles* and the exaggerated angle and height of the roof give this striking gazebo its unique look. The triangular shape of the roof is echoed in the angle of the tiered steps and the planter boxes.

Photo courtesy of Southern Pine Marketing Council

▲ *The delicate style* of the open walls and lattice roof give these twin gazebos a refined look. Built-in benches provide a comfortable place to sit while viewing sunsets on the water.

GAZEBOS

Today's gazebo can be as elaborate or as simple as you like. Open and airy, with a lattice top and just a hint of wall, or completely enclosed with a solid roof, a gazebo can function as part of the deck itself or on its own as a freestanding retreat within your yard or garden.

Photo courtesy of P & M Cedar Products

▲ *This raised gazebo* creates a more intimate area on this multi-level deck. The intricate pattern on railings of the stairway and the gazebo is an attractive design feature that visually unifies the entire deck.

FENCES, ARBORS & TRELLISES

The framework for fantastic deck design

The thin, straight boards used to make the alternating pattern of the overhead arbor work well with the rectangular shape of the space. The shape of the trellis sections makes the narrow space seem wider. ▶

▼ **The unique shape** of the arbor reflects the shape of the deck area below. The decorative railing with a built-in, angled bench adds an enclosed, intimate feeling to this separate alcove.

Fences, vertical trellises and overhead arbors are the walls and ceilings of your outdoor room. They help to buffer noise, provide privacy and control the effects of sun and wind in your deck area.

All of these structures play an integral part in the look and feel of your outdoor living space. They add beauty and establish a visual style, and should be designed to complement the related structural and visual elements in your space.

Photo courtesy of Archadeck

FENCES

Fences are as varied as the materials with which they are built. Choose a fence style appropriate to its planned use.

A recreation area should have an open fence for easy access and low-maintenance plants for minimal care. A fence around a sunbathing area should be tall and solid for privacy.

A fence can also be included strictly for decoration. A well-designed fence should reflect the style of your home and harmonize with the other elements of your outdoor living area.

Because a fence is as much a part of the neighborhood's landscape as your own, it is important to check building codes and neighborhood ordinances if you are including a fence as part of your plan.

◀ *The railing of this steep stairway works like a fence to keep the foliage back from the deck. The shape of the deck below is also defined by the railing around it.*

Photo courtesy of Western Wood Products

▲ *A tall, solid fence gives privacy to a comfortable sunbathing spot. The construction allows cooling breezes to circulate through the fence.*

Photo courtesy of Western Wood Products

▲ *You may choose to add partial fences, or a combination of fence and railing, as was done on this deck.*

Photo courtesy of Western Wood Products

▲ **The horizontal pattern** *in this fence creates a dramatic look when backlit by the sun. The pattern also is seen in other design elements of the deck.*

Photo courtesy of Western Wood Products

▲ **The attractive design pattern** *in the railing adds an artistic touch. The intricate detail acts as a screen around the deck area, and the railing serves as a privacy fence.*

▶ **Decorative railings** *throughout this redwood deck reflect the style of the deck's other structural elements, including built-in benches and overhead trellises. The rail serves as a fence, defining the deck's boundaries. The intricate pattern can be seen winding in and out of the surrounding foliage and around the perimeter of this spacious deck.*

Photo courtesy of California Redwood Assoc.

ARBORS & TRELLISES

There are a variety of styles and designs available for arbor and trellis structures. Most are made of an open-weave lattice construction that can be as intricate or simple as you like. The result is an airy structure that provides a feeling of enclosure and privacy while allowing you to enjoy the view. Arbors and trellises can also be used to support climbing plants or to camouflage unsightly objects like air conditioners, pool pumps or utility poles. An arbor or trellis is an attractive way to create a frame around a view or highlight a focal point of your deck area.

Photo courtesy of Western Wood Products

▼ *The thick beams, rounded edges and intricate latticework on this overhead arbor give a formal appearance to the dining area of this poolside deck. Outdoor lights also have been installed for nighttime use.*

Photo courtesy of California Redwood Assoc.

31

◀ **This arbor supports and frames** an attractive hanging swing, creating a comfortable place to relax and unwind.

▲ **The elaborate layered design** of this arbor includes a lowered false ceiling made of lattice material. The deck area underneath descends into an enclosed, sunken gathering area. The combination of the overhead structure and the sunken sitting area creates a private, secluded niche on this deck.

Photo courtesy of Archadeck

Photo courtesy of Western Wood Products

▲ **A small but charming** arbor with attached overhead trellis dresses up this simple garden bench.

▲ **The thin boards** and perpendicular design give this trellis an oriental look. The open design complements the other structural elements and provides a place for climbing plants to grow.

Photo courtesy of California Redwood Association

Photo courtesy of Weyerhauser

◄ *A vertical lattice panel provides privacy for deck users and conceals the shower area from the deck.*

▲ **Add a finished touch** to an ordinary deck. The lattice around the bottom covers the unsightly underside of the deck and creates a hidden storage space.

Modest use of built-in accessories creates a large, open level on this redwood deck. A flower box built around a tree has been included in the deck design. The plain benches make effective use of space and are designed to match the clean, straight line of railings.

ACCESSORIES

The Elements That Make the Difference

The accessories you use to decorate your "outdoor room" should be as multifunctional as the deck design itself. They should allow you to use your deck comfortably and conveniently in a variety of ways.

Be sure to provide places for people to sit and lounge. Benches, steps and planter boxes with wide edges provide ample seating without taking up too much space. Cooking and dining areas should include countertops and serving tables. You can also furnish your deck with customized accessories, like a built-in barbecue, fire pit or hot tub.

▶ **This deck's built-in flower box** *sits alongside the raised platform of the deck, adds interest as well as extra seating.*

Benches

▲ **Designed for optimum** use, these benches have seats on both sides. Built-in triangle-shaped flower boxes add an interesting angle.

▲ **Sturdy, wide built-in benches** follow the lines of this octagonal platform, which also includes an overhead arbor to create a shady play area.

▲ **This angled niche** is a cozy alcove—perfect for reading or relaxing.

Flower Boxes

▲ **A contemporary rectangular** shape used on the flower box and other structures on this deck creates continuity.

▲ **Benches and built-in flower boxes** form a rectangle and create a charming courtyard within a larger deck area. The flower boxes at the corners break the long benches into smaller, more comfortable, sections.

▲ **Flower boxes** built into the platform levels form a diagonal line leading up the steps.

▲ Custom-built flower boxes are incorporated into deck design; they are built as part of the bench structure, as one combined unit.

Miscellaneous

◀ **Simple lines** and shallow, terraced steps provide a place to set house plants during warm weather.

▲ A **built-in fire pit** creates a warm, cozy gathering spot on this narrow, sheltered portion of the deck. Large pillows add a splash of color and offer casual, comfortable seating.

Accessories

Photo courtesy of Archadeck

▲ **A dramatic doorway** within this outdoor living space is created when fence and arbor come together. The stylish design used in the framework on the fence panels ties into the overhead arbor and a solid pitched roof, sheltering an adjacent area.

Photo courtesy of Southern Pine Marketing Council

◀ **The furniture accessories** on this deck have a handsome design style that matches the sturdy lines of the railings and other built-in deck accessories.

Photo courtesy of Weyerhaeuser

▲ **Bench and deck** are built around an existing tree. The wraparound bench protects the tree and creates a shady sitting area or tabletop.

Photo courtesy of Georgia-Pacific Corporation

▶ **A special alcove** along the walkway of this deck houses a grill, keeping it out of the traffic area.

A Portfolio of Deck Ideas

Photo courtesy of California Redwood Association

GROUND-LEVEL DECKS

A level-headed way to handle an awkward angle

A basic, single-level deck built close to the ground can be the solution to many problems found in an outdoor environment. Narrow spaces, awkward angles and soggy ground areas are just some of the obstacles a ground-level deck can help overcome.

Whether it is attached to the house or standing alone in a far corner of the yard, a ground-level deck adds an interesting focal point to a flat, open space. Ground-level decks can be tailored to fit any size or shape, which makes them the perfect solution for filling irregular or oddly shaped areas of a yard.

An island of outdoor enjoyment, this freestanding redwood deck is an elegant place to enjoy a number of outdoor activities. A hot tub serves as the focal point of the deck. Built-in benches provide seating for socializing. An attractively tiled counter and sink area, with storage space underneath, can be used for food preparation. The lattice screen allows a gentle breeze to flow through, yet gives deck users a sense of privacy. The attractive latticework also adds an appealing backdrop, which frames the entire outdoor area.

43

GROUND LEVEL

The layout of a ground-level deck should allow easy, one-step access to and from the house. Single-level decks are often close enough to the ground that they don't need railings, although in many cases railings are still included to define boundaries and give a sense of unity to the deck setting. The ground-level decks shown here have a spacious open feeling that makes them an ideal place for sunning or entertaining.

This ground-level deck *has two open sunny spots for users to enjoy. The wide step creates an easy transition from the spacious upper level to the lawn below.* ▶

◀ *Two auxiliary deck areas,* *one with a flat, wide bench built around the edge and one with room for a table and chairs, extend from a smaller upper landing area outside a patio door. The upper area is a convenient grilling spot and has an area for storing extra chairs.*

Photo courtesy of Western Wood Products Association

Photo courtesy of Milt Charno & Associates

▲ *A large single-level deck* is detailed with a complex contemporary railing and flower box designs. The open expanse of the single-level deck is balanced by the large, two-story modern home.

▲ *The distinctive shape* of this single-level deck is enhanced with built-in planter boxes and benches. The rounded corners and decking design detail give this deck a smooth, finished line.

▲ ***This deck makes*** *effective use of a shallow space. A wide, low bench follows shape of the deck.*

◄ ***This two-tier, platform*** *deck offers an unobstructed view. The use of terraced steps allows a smooth transition from deck to yard.*

GROUND-LEVEL DECKS

Photo courtesy of Georgia-Pacific Corporation

▲ *The **flower box/bench*** combination is an intelligent and beautiful use of space on this raised deck. A deckway leads to a flat platform used for sunbathing.

Photo courtesy of Archadeck

▲ *A **single-level deck*** with simple lines surrounds this brick patio. The stain used on the deck matches the color of the patio brick, giving a unified look to the entire outdoor area.

GROUND LEVEL

▲ **An entire backyar**d is converted into an outdoor deck area. This eliminates yard maintenance and enables the designer to incorporate more
elements into the design. A diagonal style of decking design adds interest and accentuates the fire pit. This outdoor living area also includes
a gazebo and a separate dining area. A high privacy fence along the edge of the deck way provides a backdrop for the entire outdoor setting.

◀ *Four terraced levels with built-in flower boxes make up this spacious open deck. The second step down is wide enough to serve as an alternate activity area. The top area is open and bright and has a privacy fence for secluded backyard sunbathing.*

▼ *The monotony of a large, level grassy area is interrupted by a deck featuring flat, stacked levels, with clean lines and a rigid geometric design. Steps lead down to the ground level, and an arbor above a built-in corner bench provides shelter.*

TERRACED DECKS

A tiered or terraced deck is made of two or more platforms combined to create a stacked effect. A terraced deck is particularly effective in a yard with a gradual slope, where the individual tiers become gracefully decending steps. The separate tiers also can be used to define separate seating, dining and play areas—turning unusable terrain into functional outdoor living space.

GROUND-LEVEL DECKS

A graceful transition from the deck to the ground

▲ ***Slightly raised above the ground,*** *this single-level deck is at the same level as the interior floor of the house. French doors swing open to combine this roomy outdoor living area with the interior living space. A built-in bench, close to the grill, doubles as a handy table and defines a cooking and eating area.*

▲ **An elegant redwood deck** *was built into a slope and around an existing tree to create this dramatic outdoor space. An overhead arbor extends from the house across a portion of the deck, creating an enclosed, private dining area with a spectacular view. The existing tree also serves as a screen between the area under the arbor and the casual seating area at the corner.*

▼ **This single-level deck** *rests on a pedestal that extends up to meet the connecting terraced stairway. The unique pedestal base creates a circular cantilever that leaves a lot of open room underneath.*

RAISED AND MULTILEVEL DECKS

Elevated decks may rise just inches off the ground or many feet in the air. They are usually designed to extend out over a steep hillside or from a second-story patio door. Raised decks can solve the problem of a severely sloping yard by extending over and above the hard-to-reach space. High-rise decks are often elevated far enough above the ground to allow an unrestricted, sweeping view of the surroundings. The space beneath a raised deck can be used to create a cool, shaded sanctuary or it can be completely enclosed and used for storage.

▼ *Built on a drastic incline, this expansive bi-level deck sits high on stilts. A stairway leads down the steep incline to a landing that opens onto the deck area. As the stairway continues down the slope, the deck juts out from the steep hill, over the water. A spectacular, versatile deck area now takes the place of a rocky, unusable slope.*

▲ *The top platform* *of this raised deck is elevated to floor level where sliding doors provide access from a large family room. The unusual, layered design of the railings along the steps is also used in the sleek lines of the benches on the lower level.*

◀ *This enclosed, raised deck* sits *upon a beautifully finished pedestal angled at the bottom to help manage a slope in the terrain.*

Photo courtesy of Milt Charno & Associates

▲ **The raised levels** of this deck descend in a layered design, creating four separate decks linked by shallow steps. The highest level is a cantilevered deck that extends out over the lawn.

▶ **A modest deck** is adorned with a delightful overhead arbor and a bright, sunny sitting area. Wide, open steps lead down to the lawn. Lattice screen adds a decorative touch to the bottom of the deck and covers the unsightly area under the deck.

Photo courtesy of Weyerhaeuser

Photo courtesy of California Redwood Association

▲ **An elaborate raised** redwood deck accommodates many activities. A screened-in porch keeps out the insects; an open area on the upper level is perfect for sunning. A comfortable deckway becomes another activity level as needed.

Photo courtesy of Southern Pine Marketing Council

▲ **Three tiered steps** lead to the top level of this raised deck. The open platform on top creates a spacious area for playing or just relaxing and enjoying the view.

Photo courtesy of Archadeck

▲ **The steps** from the raised level lead down to a secluded patio and seating area. The built-in bench on the lower level mirrors the angled lines of the raised level.

*A **steep slope** is made into usable living area by adding an elevated deck. Existing trees are left as interesting features of the deck's surrounding scenery.* ▶

Photo courtesy of Archadeck

▼ *This **raised deck** offers a fantastic view that looks out to a scenic lake. It is private, secluded among the treetops.*

Photo courtesy of Western Wood Products

Raised levels take decks up to the wide-open spaces

▼ *The sweeping splendor of this raised deck is surrounded by a spectacular view. The simple lines of this elegant redwood deck are enhanced by a curved railing — all that's needed to add a touch of class to this natural beauty.*

▲ *This large multilevel redwood deck* sprawls down a steep hill and divides into four separate use areas with small landings between the levels. An attractive alternative to the rough terrain below the deck.

MULTILEVEL DECKS

Dividing your deck into various levels is one way to make it multifunctional. Each level serves as an individual activity area. Wide, open stairways link the levels.

The multilevel masterpieces shown on this page make the most of their sites. A steep slope, a rocky terrain and a shallow, flat expanse are transformed into outdoor living areas that are wonderfully effective, multifunctional favorites.

▲ *This expansive home* has several different deck areas extending from different rooms inside the house. The use of different levels gives each deck privacy from the others. The ground area under raised decks can also be utilized.

▲ *This deck integrates with a natural stone retaining wall* as it curves down this rocky slope. As the deck winds down the hill, different levels extend out over the steep incline. The bottom steps have a set of benches on either side of a small landing. The overgrown retaining wall behind creates a small, intimate sitting area.

▲ **Two large levels** of this multilevel deck are joined by a stairway. The lower level has a table and benches for dining and entertaining. The upper level is spacious and sunny–a perfect spot for sunbathing or for a child's play area.

▲ **This raised deck** is built above a rocky lakeshore. Wide steps from the main deck area descend to the beach. An octagonal area of the deck, used for casual dining, is two steps down and surrounded by a railing.

▲ **An expansive two-level deck** extends from both stories of this house with access to the deck from many different areas inside the home. A portion of the upper level is fully screened, making this area of the deck more useable. Lattice covers the area under the deck and creates a hidden storage space.

▲ **Delicate white lattice** is used as a design feature throughout this appealing deck. Entertain on the upper level; the lower level has a hot tub surrounded by lattice panels for privacy. The lower platform provides an area for sunning and relaxing. An overhead arbor designates a separate dining area.

Photo courtesy of Archadeck

▲ **This deck design** *makes efficient use of the area under the raised deck. The space is finished and used as a secluded place to gather with the family or quietly relax alone.*

MULTILEVEL DECKS

Make the Most of Places with Limited Spaces

▶ **The different levels** *used in this impressive addition dramatically increase the amount of usable space. The food preparation area is located on the upper level, high above and away from the dining area below. Angled stairways, with sizeable landings at each turn, link the two spaces and provide small activity areas or resting places. An attractive support column underneath the raised portion of the deck doubles as a small storage closet.*

Photo courtesy of Milt Charno & Associates

MULTILEVEL DECKS

◀ This multilevel deck *makes efficient use of a steep hillside that leads to a lakeshore. The upper deck includes an area with an overhead roof that looks out over the steep slope to the dining area on the lower level. To enjoy a scenic view of the lakeshore while dining, the lower deck area is built over the lake.*

▶ A second level *is built almost directly above the ground level to give the two areas of this deck privacy from one another. The two levels make access from inside the house much easier. A stairway leads from one level to the other.*

▼ The three levels *of this deck are connected by spiraling staircases. The angles of the deck itself are repeated in the railings and built-in benches.*

Photo courtesy of Archadeck

RECREATIONAL DECKS
Pools & Hot Tubs

Including a pool or hot tub in your outdoor living area will provide hours of fun and relaxation for your family and friends. And an outdoor pool or hot tub area is made more functional and more attractive when surrounded by a deck. The seating area around a hot tub serves many functions. Raised benches can be used for sunning, and for housing the plumbing and storing deck accessories and tools. Poolside decks need to accommodate poolside activities. They should include ample space for sunbathing and entertaining. Wooden deck surfaces drain well and create safe walkways for swimmers. Frame your poolside area with a deck to create an open, sunny spot for sunbathers.

◀ *This rooftop deck area is surrounded by a screen fence that provides privacy for hot tub users. The hot tub is enclosed by a small deck that can be used as a shelf ledge for plants or towels, or for seating in and around the hot tub. The screen shelters the deck from wind and sun but still lets through a comfortable breeze.*

Hot Tubs

▲ ***The deck area*** *that holds this octagonal hot tub overlooks a large pool area below. A railing with a built-in planter box/bench combination gives some seclusion to the hot tub area and a wide bench for sitting or lounging is built around the sunken hot tub.*

▶ ***A corner of this deck*** *juts out to create a rounded alcove with a sunken hot tub. The separate area gives hot tub users a sense of seclusion.*

▲ *A smooth, wide built-in bench* defines the hot tub area of this deck. An enclosed tub sits on one level and butts into the next level to allow access to the tub from two different levels. The smaller upper area can be used for sunning or lounging. The spacious lower level can accommodate more people. A level above the hot tub is used for cooking and is easily accessible from the house.

▲ *The lower level* of this deck area consists of large hot tub enclosed by a wood rail and an overhead arbor. Steps lead to a second or main-level walk-out deck extending from the house.

RECREATIONAL
Pools

Great for sunning and entertaining, a deck is the perfect architectural element for any poolside setting. It is important to provide a shaded area for protection from the sun. It should be roomy enough to accommodate sunbathers and outdoor furniture comfortably. Wooden poolside decking is always more comfortable to walk on because it does not get as hot as other materials.

Photo courtesy of Milt Charno & Associates

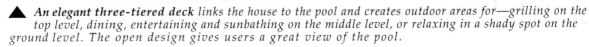

▲ *An elegant three-tiered deck* links the house to the pool and creates outdoor areas for—grilling on the top level, dining, entertaining and sunbathing on the middle level, or relaxing in a shady spot on the ground level. The open design gives users a great view of the pool.

Photo courtesy of California Redwood Association

◀ *The terraced steps* of this redwood deck wrap around an above-ground pool to give the pool a built-in feeling. They are wide enough to be used for seating or sunbathing. Sun worshippers can follow the sun as it moves down the winding steps from the upper deck level overlooking the pool.

▲ *A large raised deck* makes efficient use of the yard by creating more outdoor living space without sacrificing usable lawn area. The existing lawn under the raised deck is intact and usable. A large landing breaks the imposing stairway into two manageable sections.

◀ *Detailed decking* patterns and intricate step angles beautifully frame this hot tub setting. The high wall behind the hot tub and the angle of the tub to the house and deck create a cozy private niche for tub users. The gorgeous wood grain is seen in built-in amenities throughout the deck.

▲ *Two spacious levels* on this contemporary deck offer plenty of room for outdoor entertaining. A hot tub located on a roomy upper level has elevated privacy yet allows users a dramatic view. Below is a larger deck area with built-in benches and plenty of space for sunbathers.

RECREATIONAL

▶ **This efficient**, freestanding redwood deck has it all: a raised, sunny area for a hot tub, and a comfortable, shady dining area with an elegant arbor overhead. The attractive design links this activity area with the brick patio.

RECREATIONAL
Pools

▲ *An elegant poolside space* *includes an alfresco dining area separated from the redwood poolside deck by a slight elevation. A classic design style is used in the white wrought-iron fence and the planter and patio furniture.*

▲ *This contemporary deck* *uses black accents in the furniture and trim around the pool to contrast with the light wood in the decking and the blue colors of the water.*

▲ *A hot tub* *located in a sunny corner of this deck is the focal point for deck users. This featured area is surrounded by plenty of space for dining and entertaining, with wide built-in steps leading down to an open lawn.*

▲ *An attractive wooden decking* is cooler and safer than other materials used around pools. An open-weave lattice doubles as a decorative privacy screen and windbreak.

▲ *This raised deck* completely surrounds a ground-level pool. The deck is flush with the main level of the house. A screened-in outdoor room adds comfort from the elements, while a flat, open lawn allows you to enjoy the yard in pleasant weather.

DINING

Enjoy Eating Alfresco

A deck used for outdoor dining or cooking should be easily accessible from the kitchen. An outdoor cooking center should provide enough room to comfortably prepare food close to the grill. Tables, whether built-in or moveable, should be located conveniently close to the food preparation area, yet out of the range of blowing smoke.

Photo courtesy of Georgia-Pacific Corporation

▲ **An enclosed gazebo** *surrounds a built-in hot tub area that looks down onto another level of the deck, used for dining and socializing. These two separate areas are each sheltered by an overhead structure. All areas of this multipurpose deck are linked by decorative railings and connecting deckways.*
▼

◀ **An outdoor dining area** *is enhanced by the attractive curves in this built-in table. The curved design follows the custom curves in the deck. A contrasting decking pattern is used in the steps decending from the top level. A curved bench built around an existing tree adds extra seating options.*

DINING

Each distinct deck area should be the same size or slightly larger than an indoor room with the same function. An outdoor dining area should be approximately the same size as an indoor dining room. Be sure to allow for the fact that outdoor furniture often is larger than conventional indoor furniture.

▲ *Enjoy comfortable dining in any weather. A screened room connects to the deck area and gives the feeling of being outdoors.*

Photo courtesy of Archadeck

Photo courtesy of Southern Pine Marketing Council

▲ **This outdoor dining area** *offers users a view of an attractive enclosed hot tub alcove and other points of interest. The dining area has plenty of space for outdoor furniture and also includes built-in benches for additional seating.*

▲ **This outdoor dining area** is located close to the patio doors for easy access from inside the house. The deck area includes plenty of open space for larger social gatherings.

▼ **A small deck** with two separate areas capitalizes on efficient use of space. The design was kept simple to eliminate clutter and keep space as large as possible. Detail in railing is the only design element used.

Photo courtesy of Western Wood Products Association

▲ **Wide benches** around the outside edges of this deck accent the unusual shape and provide a comfortable spot for lounging in the sun.

◀ *The designated dining area on this large deck is easy to get to from inside the house and all areas of the deck. The casual dining atmosphere offers a view of the hot tub setting, which is enclosed by a raised deck and an overhead arbor. The grid pattern used in the decorative railing adds an art deco style to the design and also serves as a partial privacy screen.*

81

▲ **Colorful flower**s surround this very functional two-level deck. A patio door opens to lower level for easy access from the house. A raised level has plenty of room for social gatherings. A built-in bench with an interesting angle serves as a railing on the edge of the elevated deck and provides additional seating, if needed.

Entertaining

Entertaining on your deck is easy and comfortable with amenities that accommodate your guests. Save space by including structures that provide extra seating. Many bench styles and step designs can be used as comfortable seating.

▼ ***Enjoy a meal,*** *and the view, under a shady umbrella on this pleasant deck. Built around a pool, this deck has plenty of room for sunbathers and pool users alike. Built-in benches along back fence provide additional seating for social gatherings.*

MULTIPLE USES FOR YOUR DECK

The Freedom of Being Functional

A great deck is one that can accommodate many outdoor activities at one time. Careful planning and an eye for detail will give you a deck that can be used for any occasion or desired activity. Plan so that traffic flows easily from inside the home to each section of your outdoor area, and make use of amenities that perform more than one function.

▶ *This **multifunctional deck** includes an area for sunbathing, a hot tub area, an area for casual dining and a social gathering space. These activity areas are far enough apart to be used independently, or they can be integrated and used as one outdoor area.*

Photo courtesy of Archadeck

▲ ***An expansive, stylish redwood deck*** *has two spacious levels with plenty of room for large gatherings. A poolside level is open and sunny with amenities for sunbathing and outdoor dining. A lower level, three steps down, becomes a cozy spot for intimate gatherings. Wide steps lead from the lower level down through the middle of a natural stone retaining wall.*

MULTIPLE-USE DECKS

Include All the Angles

◀ **This functional deck** was designed for multiple uses. One area includes an attractive hot tub setting with a raised deck built around the tub and stylish design details used in the railings and stairways. A second dining area is conveniently located within easy access of the house and barbecue. As an attractive and functional built-in feature, a long bench follows the edge of the ground level and doubles as a railing.

▲ **A lower-level courtyard** is one small part of this multiple-use deck. This shady, quiet area is surrounded by colorful flowers. The interesting triangle-shaped flower boxes add a point of interest and separate the long, connected benches.

MULTIPLE USES
Multifunctional Favorites

▼ **This expansive deck** *includes two or three large areas, each with multiple uses. A raised deck in back, a sunken courtyard area to the right of the terraced area, and a large dining area on the top level of the deck can each function as a separate activity area. All areas can also be united to form one multifunctional area for large social gatherings.*

▲ **Higher level** overlooks a lovely courtyard, built around a large shade tree. The terraced steps have a built-in combination bench/flower box that also sets off the courtyard.

MULTIPLE USES

Photo courtesy of Western Wood Products Association

▲ *A hard-to-maintain, narrow space is now a multifunctional deck way that can be used for a number of activities. A fire pit surrounded by a diamond-style decking pattern is the center of one area. The diagonal direction of the decking pattern leads to an open dining area.*

Photo courtesy of California Redwood Association

◀ *This spectacular redwood deck is divided into intimate and cozy corners. One distinct alcove includes a sunken dining area located under an elaborate gazebo. The existing trees have been integrated as design elements.*

MULTIPLE USES

▶ *A modest ground-level deck* can be used effectively in a small space. A sunny hot tub area invites sun worshippers to enjoy the deck, while shade lovers can enjoy the natural beauty on a comfortable shaded bench.

◀ *Even small outdoor areas* can be multifunctional. In this open, sunny deck area a solid fence creates privacy for sunbathers, a secure area for children to play or a secluded spot for dining and entertaining.

▼ *A separate cantilevered deck area
extends this portion of the deck out over
a steep slope, creating a scenic overlook. The
remaining deck area is spacious and usable
for many outdoor activities. A short, wide
box structure built around a tree becomes
a built-in bench.*

Photo courtesy of Southern Pine Marketing Council

◀ **An open deck area** *around a pool is a hot spot for sun worshippers. The attractive lattice provides privacy while a refreshing breeze flows through the open weave. The simple lines of the decking pattern complement the intricate detail of the latticework.*

▶ **The simple lines** *of this small deck have a multifunctional appeal. The terraced steps double as seating or can be used to hold plants and other decorative deck embellishments. The open design offers a sunny place to relax with a clear view from the top. Even a modest deck can increase the value of your outdoor living space.*

Photo courtesy of Western Wood Products Association

Photo courtesy of Georgia-Pacific Corporation

Multifunctional

▲ **The deck area around this hot tub**, with the addition of built-in benches, was designed to save space. A raised deck built around the tub gives it its own small alcove for privacy. The hot tub area is connected to, and is easily accessible from, other levels and activity areas of this deck.

LIST OF CONTRIBUTORS

We'd like to thank the following design companies, trade associations and manufacturers of deck and wood treatment products for providing the photographs used in this book:

Archadeck®
U.S. Structures, Inc.
2112 West Laburnum Ave.
Richmond, VA 23227
(800) 722-4668

Caddcon Designs, Inc.
4707 O'Donnell Street
Baltimore, MD 21224
(800) 821-DECK

California Redwood Association
405 Enfrente Drive, Suite 200
Novato, CA 94949
(415) 382-0662

Milt Charno & Associates, Inc.
611 North Mayfair Road
Wauwatosa, WI 53226
(414) 475-0881

Georgia-Pacific Corporation
133 Peachtree Street NE
P.O. Box 105605
Atlanta, GA 30348-5605
(404) 521-4000

Kop-Coat, Inc.
Wolman® Protection
Products Division
Koppers Building K1824
Pittsburgh, PA 15219
(800) 556-7737

P & M Cedar Products, Inc.
P.O. Box 7349
Stockton, CA 95267
(209) 957-6360

Southern Pine Marketing Council
P.O. Box 641700
Kenner, LA 70064-1700
(504) 443-4464

Western Wood Products Association
Yeon Building, 522 SW Fifth Avenue
Portland, OR 97204-2122
(503) 224-3930

Weyerhaeuser
P.O. Box 189
R.D. #2 Campbell Road
Titusville, PA 16354
(800) 553-5759